DIVORCING

THE GAME

My Journey from the Stripper Pole

to Owning a Million-Dollar Trucking Business

To: Madge

Ashley

ASHLEY THOMAS

PRAISES FOR
DIVORCING THE GAME

Wow—I read up to 3 paragraphs. This is a powerful story of a young woman who thought she wasn't wanted, who thought no one cared, who thought she didn't have a mother or father who even cared for her. Isn't it wonderful and powerful to know that we were wanted before we ever existed? That our story was created before we were? We have a loving Father who watches out for our day and night, who has a powerful plan to reach others—others whose stories may be similar to Ashley's. I believe most of us have been rejected in one way or another either from parents, friends, supervisors, or just plain people. We've felt that strong rejection that could have overwhelmed us to doing diabolical things to ourselves, but our purpose was revealed to us right on time! I am grateful that Ashley is using that sense of rejection to cover and hug those with the loving arms of God. To whisper that they, too, have a purpose to reach those who have the same feeling of uselessness and move them towards re-visiting their purpose! -Dr. Cassandra Bradford

DIVORCING THE GAME is a read I found extremely compelling in light of the openness and truthful personal expression. It was moving and is a true portrait of today's young women that are victims of the erosion of family in America today. -Micheal Johnson

Just reading chapter 1 of the game, you can already tell the rest of the book will be phenomenal. Oftentimes we see people's success and we don't know the hell they went through to get there. I'm sure that 7-year-old girl who sat on her grandmother's porch never thought that she would have such a wonderful life and inspiring others. This is true out of the trenches story. When she said, I never lost my value or my title in God's eyes. I felt that deep in my soul. We let our struggles beat us down so badly that we lose our worth. Her story shows that no matter the circumstances you will make it through.
-Sheena Clark

Ashley, all I can say is OMG! When we first met and you told me your story. I knew right then I had to help you tell it. Thank you for changing my life! A MUST read for everyone!
- Willie Tubbs

Ashley's vulnerability about her flaws and mistakes make you feel as though you're seeing yourself reflected. This book will inspire you to be true to yourself. It's her own Cinderella story... great read. -Tonya Griffin

CONTENTS

DEDICATION

I want to thank the Almighty God & my great-grandmother, Ione Henry. I thank God for allowing my granny to be available to take me in and instill the Word of God in me. I thank you for building me up to be the woman I am today. Now I realize you were hard on me because you were the one who believed in me the most.

To my students, thank you for allowing me to coach you to success. I am very proud of each of you for mashing the gas with the tools provided to you and executing the mission.

To the leaders, Adam Wingfield, Michael Johnson, and Dr. Cassandra Bradford, thank you for the mentorship you all provided to assist me with unlocking new levels.

Thank you to my spiritual coach, Willie Tubbs, for the discipleship and holding my hand through writing this book to change the world. I am so grateful that you saw something special in my pain and pushed me to another dimension. The prayers, late-night masterminding, and the work you invested in this project is much appreciated. If you are interested in RESETTING your life with Coach Wille Tubbs, you can find him at Agents of Change LLC (agentsofchangenetwork.com).

I want to thank Saadiq Shabazz for being there for me day and night through this thing called life. You are my soon-to-be husband, and I appreciate everything you do. You keep me on my toes and supported me throughout this rough journey of creating this book to bring other people out of the trenches, and I am forever grateful. Thank you for taking care of me the best way you know how, and thank you for being my Clyde because I'm definitely your Bonnie.

And to my God and Savior, I am so thankful that You trusted me with the vision and dream to help create a movement that changed the world for the greater good. I am honored to be the chosen walking testimony in the flesh of Your great works. Please continue to use me, Lord, for Your Glory, and I will continue to be obedient. I love you! Now, let's get to work!!!

Chapter 1

Where Are You?

Growing up as a young child, I didn't understand where my parents were and why I was being taken care of at my great-grandmother's house. One thing I want you guys to understand is the value of being a king's kid.

One day, I saw something on social media that instantly caught my attention. It was crazy because I really don't scroll through Instagram that much because of my work schedule. But I was scrolling, scrolling, scrolling, and I saw this pastor stomping on money—I mean, STOMPING! STOMPING! I said to myself, "Hold on! Let me rewind!!" Like, *what's going on?* He was stomping on that money, and he was asking a young woman, probably about eighteen or nineteen years old, whom he had brought up to the stage, if she wanted the twenty dollars on which he was stomping.

"Yes," the girl replied.

The pastor then started rumpling the money. "Do you still want this money?"

"Yes, of course! I want the money," she replied.

The pastor then trampled upon the twenty-dollar bill again. I mean, it was a hot mess. He was just stompin' and stompin'. He almost ripped it up!

He asked her one last time, "Do you still want this money, girl?"

"YES!"

"Because it never lost its value!! That's why you want that twenty-dollar bill, baby—because it never lost its value! So just because you took a hit, Queen, doesn't mean you lost your value. I know you've been beaten. I know you've been bruised. I know you've been twisted. I know you've been thrown down time after time, but you still got value because I still have mine, because we are a King's kid!"

> You have something SPECIAL! You have greatness within you! You can do more than you can ever IMAGINE!!
> -Les Brown

Life has stomped on me, chewed me up, and spit me out, but I never lost my value or my title in God's eyes. *Where are you? Where are you?* Do y'all remember when God asked Adam and Eve that same question? *Where are you?*

Adam and Eve were in the Garden of Eden, and all was good. They ate the fruit of the Garden in abundance. That's where they were. But when they sinned against God, they began to cover themselves up. Ain't that something?

So, to my readers, let me ask you again: Where are you? Where are you mentally? Where are you physically? Where are you spiritually? If you're in the trenches, is there a way out? Is there truly a way out of the trenches?

If you are a believer, you have to understand your position as God's Child. You're amazing and wonderfully made, and you have power and value because you never lost it, no matter how hard you took a hit.

When I was nine months old, my mother, the person that carried me in her womb, dropped me off on my great-grandmother's porch in a car seat, rang the doorbell, and never came back to take care of me and to love me. Where was she? Why didn't she want me? Where was my dad? Why didn't he want me?

Little did they know, and who even knows if they know to this day, that dropping me off at nine months and ringing that PARTICULAR doorbell at that PARTICULAR time was the BEST decision they could have ever made for my life.

Where was my mom? I would often argue with my great-grandmother about where my mom was and would say things like, "I just want to be with my mom! You're trying to keep me away from her!" I was blind to the fact that she loved me and wanted the best for me and that I had been left by the two that made me.

My mother was on drugs. I'll never forget the name of the clown who introduced my mom to drugs. Ol' Pumpkin turned her onto crack cocaine. From there, it went downhill. Now, let's get to my dad; where was he? My dad was such a player and worried about smashing women instead of worrying about the little girl he left at my great-grandmother's house as well. He was just as guilty as my mother.

My dad left me there because he would rather be a player and deal with this woman or that one. I would often sit outside on the porch, looking up and down the street on the days that he was supposed to come and get me. Most of the time, my great-grandmother and my papa would come outside on the porch when the streetlights came on and say, "Ashley, you know what? Come on in, baby. He's not coming." That stuck with me, and that put a burning desire in me to where once I got older, I never wanted to be rejected. I never wanted to feel like I wasn't good enough. See, my mother and father made me feel like I wasn't good enough. *If I was so good, how could you leave me? How could you not care?* I felt they didn't want me. I felt I didn't deserve their love.

I believed whatever was out in the streets was way more important to my parents than I was. But again, little did they know, I never lost my value. The best thing they could have ever done for my life was leave me in the hands of somebody that had the Spirit of the Living God in them to pour into me. It was a blessing in the disguise of pain.

And you know, it's crazy because, at the age of probably six or seven, I was playing outside in the front yard with the neighbors' kids. Randomly, my mom pulls up, and she starts an argument with my great-grandmother and papa and snatches me and puts me in the truck with her.

So, all of a sudden, you now want to come back and get your child? For what? What's the purpose? Because you got a new man, a new millionaire, a new somebody who sees something in you and is mad at you because you don't have your child? Is that the only reason you came back for me? So, you snatched up your child and drove off. You were already on drugs, and you'd been hiding it from the guy you'd been dating. With your seven-year-old daughter that you barely even know in the car with you, you roll up the windows, light up your crack pipe, and drive off into the sunset like everything's okay, like you just hadn't stolen me.

We get to the destination you're taking me to, which was the drug dealer's house that you scored from. Two days later, my granny found me at that crack house, where I was left in some random man's bed with my mother nowhere to be found.

After that, I grew up to despise my great-grandmother because after she found me, I couldn't play outside anymore or have any type of freedom until I was a teenager; I still barely had it then.

So, now I'm turning into a young woman, around twelve or thirteen years old. I couldn't have any type of freedom with my friends because my great-grandmother was still afraid my mom would steal me again, so I had hell to pay for my mom's actions. So, now, where am I?

My childhood was stolen from me, and to fuel the fire of pain inside of me is to know they already didn't want me. But my mom still found a way to pull that stunt when she snatched me, and it scared my great-grandmother badly.

So, you didn't want me, and you stole my childhood from me? Why? Where am I? Where am I?

PRAYER: Heavenly Father, I express my gratitude to You for keeping me in a secret place, planting me and watering me even through the pain. I thank You for not allowing destruction to prosper even though the weapon was formed. I ask that You continue to keep Your hand on me and guide me along the best pathway of my life. In Jesus' name, I love You..Amen

CHAPTER 2

THE GAME (GO AND MONETIZE EVERYTHING)

See, I remember *The Players Club* movie. I know most of you have seen it, especially if you got this book in hand! But the question is, have you really paid attention to the principles in that movie for real, instead of just T&A...? One thing Diamond said that I'll never forget is, "I love The Players Club for offering women a way to restart goals in life. But I also hated The Players Club for the girls that were destroyed in the process." I'll never forget that!

> Respect yourself enough to walk away from anything that no longer serves you, grows you or makes you happy.
> -Grant Cardone

But when I stepped into that lifestyle as a fourteen-year-old woman in the making, I looked up to Diamond, as crazy as it may sound, because that's what it was! A crazy way of thinking. I was ready to become a woman, and that's what I really thought a woman was: Money, Power, and Respect.

I remember sneaking and watching that movie back in 1998 when I was only ten years old. I had to sneak because my great-grandmother definitely wasn't allowing that in her house. And now, as an adult, I understand exactly why. The why was so I wouldn't fall into the mouth of the game, like Ebony. I say Ebony, not Diamond, because I thought I knew how to handle myself. But later, I was unexpectedly wrong.

I admired Diamond in the movie. How classy she was. Even in a room full of wolves, she still held her dignity like a lady, even when she degraded herself. I wanted to be like her. She was the ideal stripper in my eyes. She was beautiful, confident, and smart. But, unfortunately, my story wasn't like hers. I was more like her cousin, Ebony; you know, the inexperienced one that thought she knew everything about the game but ended up in the belly of the game. Thank you to my great-granny for instilling the Word of God in me at such a young age because, without it, I wouldn't have survived what was to come. So, low-key, she saved my life. But all I can say is, "But God ..." He is the only explanation of why I'm still alive.

I am truly a walking testimony of God's grace and mercy. You won't understand why I say that until later in this book. My journey to the nightlife started when I dropped out of the ninth grade and ran away from my great-grandmother's house. I found my biological mother at a sleazy motel she was living in. I manipulated her and told her a whole bunch of lies so she would let me stay for the little time I needed to come up with a master plan. I was a hustler, and I knew that with my hustler's ambition and my hustle mindset, I would come up with a plan, because I was not going back to my great-grandmother's house.

That was not an option because I felt imprisoned, and I was itching to see the world my granny was keeping me from. Paradise, right? That's what she was keeping me from. It had to be, because she was sheltering me. She was sheltering me from it way too tough! She didn't want me to have fun, right? She didn't want me to enjoy my teenage years.

Right? That had to be the case. There couldn't be any other reason in my mind at the time. I was so damn naive! It would come back later to slap me in the face.

So, my mom left to do her daily hustle so she could keep paying for the low-budget hotel we were living in for another night. So, I was left alone with only my crafty thoughts and myself to think of a quick fix. A little voice in my mind told me that since my mom was into street life, there had to be something in that room to give me a clue. *There's got to be something in this room to give me a solution.* So, I began to take action until I found what I was looking for.

I rummaged through my mom's room, and lo and behold, I found a magazine that looked like the *Green Sheet*. But the difference about this *Green Sheet* was that it had the image of a half-naked woman on it. It intrigued me because, at an early age, I knew the power of a woman's body—sex and money. I found this out in ninth grade when a popular pastor would often pick me up from school and molest me. I looked through that green-sheet-type of paper I found, with different women in it who said they charged different amounts for a girlfriend experience, and saw a now-hiring post.

The ad looked so professional. I knew this had to be legit, and it had to be a lick. It seemed like my way out! I knew this was the quick way that I was looking for. It was advertised as an escort service for high-end clients only. So, you know, my young mind thought, *okay, cool. I can make that type of money in an hour going to dinner with old men and keeping them company.* But little did I know, my fast ass would hear the same words Dollar Bill said in *The Players Club* just a few days later: "You get what I give you. I got a contract between me and you that tells you to do what I tell you to do. Therefore, shut the fuck up. Don't say nothing. Don't even look at me. I'll tell you what.. you better get up out of my office and get out of my face before your ass gets swollen." That's when I learned: make the money; don't let it make you.

I fell deep into the pits of the nightlife.

Nightlife is one of the biblical meanings of the valley of the shadow of death. Remember, this book is only for the people who have gone through something in life, not the churchy folks who have never done anything wrong or never gone through anything.

Now, for my people who have been through something, I know you have heard the famous scripture, Psalms 23, verses 1 through 4, "The Lord is my shepherd. I shall not ever be in want. He restores my soul. He guides me in the path of righteousness for his name's sake. And even though I walk through the valley of the shadow of death, I will fear no evil, for you are with me; your rod and your staff, they comfort me." That is where I was when I called that phone number on the now-hiring ad—at the valley of the shadow of death. I didn't even realize it. I was on the devil's playground.

Have you ever heard that loud, manipulating voice telling you to do wrong by giving you excuses to justify your decision when something goes wrong? Or better yet, how many times have you ignored the voice that comes right after that voice, telling you that you're stepping into dangerous territory and you need to go back? Be honest. Again, I'm not talking to the churchy people who have never been through anything. Listen to the voice that tells you the same thing Dollar Bill said in *The Players Club* movie: "IT'S GONE BE TROUBLE! TROUBLE!!" You better listen to it! That's just what it is! I jumped into that lifestyle, and by the grace and the mercy of

God, I made it out of the game! Remember, Kings and Queens, most don't make it out. Don't get caught up in the common phrase they would always tell you: "I'm not trying to turn you out ... I'm just trying to turn you on to some game!"

Later that night, after I took the next step and called the now-hiring phone number on that ad in that magazine, or the "Prostitute Green Sheet" (which I would later discover), a brand-new, black, drop-top Corvette—I'm talking brand new—pulled up to pick me up. I had no idea that my life would never be the same once I got into that Corvette. I had no idea as a thirteen-year-old child that I was stepping into the world of sex trafficking. I "thought" I was just going to be fashionable and cute with older rich men at parties, but boy was I wrong. So, here we go. I hope y'all ready for this story.

PRAYER: Heavenly Father, I come to You right now and I thank You for your grace and mercy for covering me when Sata n tried to steal my life. When he thought I was walking alone in the valley of the shadow of death, You were with me, and I am forever grateful. Thank You, Jesus, for covering me, even in the multiple unexplainable situations. I did not end up dead, and people didn't understand that the evidence of Your presence was and is continuously with me. I'm forever grateful and honored that You chose me out of all people to be a testimony of the evidence of Your works. Thank you. In Jesus' name I pray. Amen.

CHAPTER 3

RENEGADE

Ladies, have you ever realized that the strip club is a dream-selling business? You have to be aware of those men if you plan on making it out of the trenches. Let me tell you this story about a beautiful little thirteen-year-old chocolate girl. She told me she ran away and left the house for good because she had no freedom. Her mother was stealing her, and she was running away. She didn't have a childhood, so she felt like she had to get out there to live. She fell into the hands of a pimp, at the age of thirteen, looking for jobs in *A&E Magazine* ads, the same magazine she found in her mother's sleazy hotel room, because she had left the house and needed a way to make a living. So, she called a number in the "Hiring" section, and a woman named Chyna answered and scheduled an interview.

Chyna pulls up to the sleazy hotel in a brand-new Corvette! Black-on-black drop top! She fell in love with that car! Little Chocolate hops in, and off they go. Chyna takes her to Budget Suites and introduces her to several other women and a sixty-year-old man, "The Pimp." All the women were beautiful, dressed nice, and rolling in luxury vehicles! So, the little chocolate girl stays and pushes to make the sixty-year-old pimp happy. She needed clothing, shelter, and food. She stays there for two months, making money and all that, paying him 60 percent of everything she brings in.

This little girl was a real piece of work. She did all she could do to pull her weight and make the pimp happy so she could get a Corvette one day soon. Then comes a knock on the door. She's living with four or five girls—you know, older women in their twenties and thirties that are working for him as well. So, she feels comfortable opening the door, and BOOM!! It's a robbery! The men in masks kicked in the door and passed by her because she couldn't move. They wouldn't say what they wanted. They pulled out guns and said, "This is a robbery. Where's your pimp because we want all his money!" And you know what? God spared her life because this little girl had so much favor over her life!

One of the robbers looked at the little girl as he pointed a gun at the other escorts in the house. He looked at her and said, "You're cute. We're not going to kill you. But I do want your number. I'm going to call you as soon as I get situated." God spared her life, and the robbers left. Luckily, nobody was hurt.

The robbers called the pimp's phone later. They said, "Hey, that little pretty young thing that you had in the house, where is she? I want to talk to her." Everybody looked at the little chocolate girl like she had set them up. This innocent little girl was in danger. She just wanted to please somebody because of the rejection from her parents, so she wouldn't have dared to set them up. That's what happens when you're caught up in the lion's den in the trenches.

The rejection stayed a long time with this little chocolate thirteen-year-old girl. So, the little girl ran off. She ran away because they were going to kill her—they thought she had set the pimp up. So, she left there and got her own place. After she had got her own place, she booked an appointment with a client by herself. She thought she could do escorting alone as a young kid with no security, no pimp, no sister wives, no nothing. She had her first date. He came in there, and he was a handsome young man. He looked like a football player. He came in and asked if he could use the restroom. She led him there, and once she turned around, he pulled out a gun and raped her from front to back. He almost took her life. But still, she never lost her value.

The trenches is a weird space to be in, and I'm talking to those that have been through something. This book isn't for the ones that haven't been through anything. This is for those who have been beaten, bruised, twisted, stomped on, and all of that! The ones who need to find value and awareness as the children of the King, to make it out of the trenches and truly divorce the game in the strip club, street life, and the dope-selling lifestyle.

After the rape, I knew I couldn't stay trapped in the sex-trafficking mentality created in me as a little girl. If I had continued on that path, I would have been dead soon playing on those grounds. I took another route and got a fake ID from someone and got a job at a strip club. I was a kid, still walking on the cliff of the pits of hell. I stayed in the belly of the strip club up until I was twenty-four years old. That's all I knew, and I was trapped in that life.

Thank God, I met a guy I dated for a few years at twenty-four years old, who gave me an ultimatum. He said, "Look, Ashley, I'm going to help you find a respectable job because I can't have you on my arm while you're stripping for other men. You are running with the wrong crowd and ruining your life and reputation." I honored that because I knew he was right. It was time for a dramatic shift in my life for the better. I agreed, and he stood by his word and found me a job at an alarm company. I stayed there for four years and was the top rep because I already had a sales mentality from what I had been through.

Listen, guys, I had to figure it out. You have to STOP linking up with the wrong crowds! Show me your friends, and I'll show you your future. Linking up with the wrong crowds will destroy you because the devil comes to kill, steal, and destroy, and that's the fastest way to go nowhere fast.

Ladies, let me ask you a question: How many times have you felt devalued? How many times have you left the strip club—or even off the track for a pimp—and you looked at your money and the bankroll that you made for the night and just cried? Just ask yourself, how many times? How many times have you felt filthy after getting off stage or sleeping with a man because you needed the money? How many times?

Heavenly Father, we come to you today and express our gratitude first and foremost. I thank You for everything You have done even if You don't do anymore. I am thankful and grateful to be Yours. I plead the blood of Jesus over all of the readers of this book and that you dispatch their angels and place a hedge of protection over them Oh God. We thank you, Lord, for Your mercy and grace and the lives that you're touching through this message. I am so honored for you to allow me to be a used vessel in your active ministry. in Jesus' Name. AMEN

CHAPTER 4

OPERATION WORK

Let's talk about working on reaching kingship. There comes a time when everyone, at some point in life, reaches out to someone else for help, especially in an area of expertise. That's unfamiliar territory to them. You know the saying, "I don't need help from anyone." I know you hear that a lot. "I'm good. I don't need anybody." Well, I'm here to tell you that everyone needs someone, no matter what. You don't believe me? Well, I will prove it to you with a few scenarios. Rappers need producers.

Doctors need patients. Architects need clients, and drug dealers need clients and plugs. So, to me, self-made is a myth.

In August 2017, I found the territory I was walking in to be very unfamiliar when my great-grandmother, landlord, and I dove headfirst into the trucking industry. Let me take y'all back to 2015 when God rescued me from the street life I was trapped in—that way, y'all can feel what I'm talking about.

I was at the after-hour club at about 5:00 a.m., kickin' it, partying, and all that, when the Holy Spirit told me to drive to the church. Man, I was like, "What? Here I am right now, drunk Lord, in stiletto heels and a freakum dress. I ain't going to no church!" It was amusing to me that a thought like that would ever cross my mind while I was having a twerk-off. So, I told the Holy Spirit "No," but then, He got louder and louder in my spirit to get to work.

I finished my cup of Hennessy and walked out to my Jaguar in the parking lot. I sat in the car, drunk as hell, and meditated on the fact that I was really about to look crazy by driving to the church and parking until service started. Remember, y'all, it's 5:00 a.m., so the church had yet to start service. They didn't start until 9:00 a.m. The Holy Spirit pulled on me so hard. And God said, "Go." So, I went. I actually went to the church house, parked, and got in my backseat drunk as a skunk and passed out.

The sun was up and beaming, and I can't tell you if a church member, the pastor, or God woke me up, but I know I made it to service on time with my freakum dress on, stilettos and all. Can you imagine what I'm telling you? Picture that; it was a description of Matthew 11: 28, "Come to me all you who are weary and burdened, and I will give you rest." I knew I needed rest but didn't feel too keen about that scripture. The moment I stepped into the church, God spoke differently, though—I was an exclusive guest of His.

That bright and early Sunday morning, I sat in the church, still drunk. I hear stories from church members about me screaming, "God, give me the power! God, give me the power!" And I was loud. So funny, right?

But what's not funny is that my soul was crying out to God. That same Word of God, which my great- grandmother instilled in me, was burning to get out the phrase "Give me the power!" It was a full eyeopener to me. I fell in love with God that Sunday morning while looking like a prostitute, and it was an honor to be God's exclusive guest that morning. I've never felt so invited and comforted.

The people who looked at me thought I had lost my damn mind, but again, when you're a guest of the Almighty God, you don't need validation from any flesh and blood walking this earth. He was and is my only concern.

The church is for the sick, and we, as God's people, need to understand that. I'm gonna repeat that. The church is for the sick, and we, as God's people, need to understand that. What if I felt embarrassed when the women of the church were whispering and snarling at me? What if I had left? Where would I be now? I understand why people want God without a church experience now, because people have made the church experience so bad.

I thank God for giving me the courage not to leave. The pastor told me years later that the first day he saw me, I showed him what a made-up mind looks like. Have you heard the new saying that entrepreneurs talk about? What is it they say?? Oh yeah, "All I need to do is get in a room. If I could just get in the room!!!!" But I'm here to tell you that I was God's VIP guest at the church that morning. So, no matter what people thought about me, I felt like Megan Thee Stallion. "No, you can't touch this, ayeee."

No, for real though, God had a special shield around the kid.

No one would believe what I did the next weekend after I left church that Sunday. I was back in the club that Saturday, but only to tell the people in the club what the Bible says in John 14:6, "Jesus answered, I am the way, the truth and life. And no one comes to the father, except through me." I told everyone in the club that Jesus was the way and, after the club was over, to pull up to the church so they could be delivered as well. It was mind-blowing to see half of the club in the church house that Sunday morning. You don't know the joy I felt telling the people in darkness, literally in darkness inside of a nightclub, that God delivered me from there, and He could do the same for them if they would just trust Him. The pastor saw all the newcomers and didn't know what was going on. The look on people's faces were priceless. And I didn't tell anyone in there that those people were my guest. I wasn't gonna take credit for the movement of God.

I was happy that, of all people, God chose me to be a vessel He could utilize. God called me to assist Him at a nightclub. Who would've imagined? From that moment, I decided to trust God all the way. Even when my lights went out, stripping and running back to the streets were no longer options. I knew the presence of God was with me the morning I woke up in my apartment and noticed that my lights were turned off. Because I had let the street life go, I had no income. A subtle voice said to me, "Do not worry. Go back to sleep.

Everything's gonna be fine." So, I listened and fell back into a deep sleep. It seems like when God tells you to go back to sleep, you fall into the best deep sleep ever. There is something about the saying, "Everything is gonna be fine." He said it, and I listened.

When I woke up, I could see that the lights had been turned back on, and they never got cut off again.

Do y'all hear what I'm saying? I trusted God when I decided never to go back to street life. So, please understand that He will do the same for you. He has my back, and I love Him. I felt His presence that day in the nightclub, and I've been chasing it ever since. I chase him daily because He saved my life.

Prayer: Heavenly Father, we come to You today with gratitude in our hearts. We thank You for not allowing Sata n to take us out when he tried to. We thank You for your continuous love, mercy, and grace. We thank You for guiding us, for being a comforter to us. Our Father, who are in heaven, hallowed by thy Name, thykingdom come, thy will be done, on earth as it is in heaven. Give us this day our daily bread. And forgive us of our trespasses, as we forgive those who trespasses against us.And lead us not into temptation, but deliverus from evil. For thine is the kingdom, and the power, and the glory, for ever and ever.

In Jesus' name we pray. Amen.

CHAPTER 5

MWG (MIGHTY WOMAN OF GOD)

Let me tell you guys a story about a sharecropper's daughter I met, who was born in the '30s. I know it's 2021, so for those who don't know what a sharecropper is, let me tighten you up real quick. The definition of a sharecropper: they lived on land owned by an individual called landowners. They let the blacks live ontheir land in exchange for them to grow their crop as rent. The landowners still got crops and money, even though they didn't work for it—basically slavery. This woman inspired me in such a major way. She came all the way from Fairfield, TX, to Fort Worth, TX, in Stop Six. She is gorgeous inside and out, and she showed me the real definition of a queen. So, I never understood how a woman that really came from literally nothing could have such a positive outlook on life.

It's almost fictional the things that she went through—anunexplainable type of pain.

> Stop running from your pain and embrace your pain. Your pain is going to be a part of your prize, a part of your product. I challenge you to push yourself. -Eric Thomas

It's funny how our new generation constantly complains and complains about our current situations. Here, this woman sat on the floor as a child and had to drink out of a tuna and spam aluminum can because they couldn't afford drinks, cups, or chairs. It's so selfish how we can sit and—I emphasize the word inaction—not do shit when we have all the resources to change our situation with action nowadays. She hated every minute of her situation, but she didn't quit or give up hope like so many of us do today. She suffered, but she was determined to live the rest of her life as a champion, no matter what her current situation was, no matter what she saw as reality.

This woman knew the reality in her mind, and it was an intense dog fight. She also knew she would and could make it with God's dependable direction, grace, and guidance. She knew the only way to get out of the mediocracy was to keep shooting for the stars. So, as a sharecropper's daughter, she knew it was more to life than poverty, especially when she saw her cousin Sane come around after they moved from Fairfield, Texas, to Fort Worth.

Cousin Sane pulled up in a burgundy Cadillac, wearing a fur coat in the summertime because she had that bankroll after bankroll like Lil' Boosie. She had that bankroll all year round. Cousin Sane pulled up to funky town in a $600 mink coat at the time, and this was over seventy years ago, y'all. So you know, black folks weren't rocking that type of "drip." So, Cousin Sane was lit, really. I don't know about y'all, but when I see someone doing big things, that shit inspires me. This lady had that dog in her. She had the dog fight in her, and it was activated when she saw Cousin Sane.

Cousin Sane had a street in Como, TX, with houses that looked like tiny little huts that she rented out to the people in the hood at an affordable price. This lady was on her shit for real! When her baby cousin saw those huts, her wealth mindset was born. She saw that burgundy Cadillac, the clothes, the mink fur, and the caddy—all that. And no blacks had mink, caddies, or real estate. That's when the little girl realized that she could do anything she set her mind to because her cousin came from being dirt poor too. Dirt poor, y'all; visualize what I'm telling you.

When I'm talking about dirt poor, that's not living in the projects; that's coming from nothing for real, for real. Cousin Sane bought a block in the hood in Como, TX. She hired a new carpenter and put five hut rental properties on it with no concrete, just muddy streets. She literally came from nothing. That's how she finished but not how she got started. She didn't want to pick any more cotton, y'all. Y'all wouldn't know anything about that. Do you hear me? I said cotton picking! She had to be phenomenal and create her own lane or be forgotten. This is why I don't respect excuses, period. I don't respect them.

The people who have the advantage in today's age with excuses are poor. Yeah, you heard me ... poor. The definition of poor to me is "Passing over opportunities repeatedly." I've seen it too many times. Most people don't want to succeed as badly as they want to breathe. Now I understand what Eric Thomas meant when he said, "When you want to succeed as bad as you want to breathe, then you'll be successful." That shit is true and real, no matter if you want to believe it or not. It's real; that's your choice. Just don't find yourself making excuses while passing over opportunities repeatedly. Focus on the twenty-four hours you have today and do what you can to get closer to where you want to be. One day will be your day! Write that down now. Put it in your affirmations journal. One day will be your day! You have to be intentional about what you want to do each day; make it efficient.

> *Your excuses might be legit but they won't improve your life.*
> *-Grant Cardone*

So, where is the sharecropper's daughter now? The same one that drank out of spam cans because she had no cups. Where is she? Well, today, she is ninety years old, sitting on a bankroll because she went after her dreams and followed God's voice to get to her destination. Trust God, y'all, and try Him for yourself. Not just because I'm telling you about Him; try Him for yourself. That same woman heard her doorbell ring and opened the door and saw a nine-month-old baby in a car seat on her front porch. A car drove off, not looking back, with the driver saying, "Watch my baby." It was more like, "Here's your package." She is the mighty woman of God who raised me. She taught me never to give up, despite my current reality, but to go for my dreams. Yes, my reality was fucked up because I felt abandoned by my mother and father. Little did they know, that was the best decision they could have ever made for my life.

When I was dropped off on the porch of that mighty woman of God, my life started because she spoke life into me and instilled the Word of God in me as a toddler. That saved my life, so she is truly my superhero.

My great-grandmother now has multiple properties that she rents out, just like Cousin Sane. She's in the trucking industry and supports me in everything. Who would have ever imagined that a sharecropper's daughter born in the 1930s would follow her dreams and is now living her dream out with God's presence still radiating all over her? Who would have ever imagined? She's the first millionaire in our family. Who would have ever imagined that from a sharecropper's daughter?

To my readers, real talk, y'all. If God can do it for a sharecropper's daughter and an abandoned child, a thirteen-year- old runaway, a former stripper who fell into the hands of a pimp as a teenager, then what makes you think He can't do it for you? Again, what makes you think He can't do it for you? I want you to dig down deep and find out the answer to that question, because God has got it if only you would let Him into your heart. He's a gentleman, y'all, who stays true to His promise. I speak from direct experience.

Everyone needs to be inspired to know that the sky is the limit—because it definitely is. I encourage y'all to keep pushing because it's right on the other side of the door if you stay down. 1 Thessalonians 5:11, "Therefore encourage and build one another up, just as you were already doing."

PRAYER: Heavenly Father, I come to You boldly at the throne of grace, and I thank You for peace, Your Holy Spirit, and Your strength, especially when I am weak. I thank You for sending Your Holy Spirit to Your people as a Helper and as a Comforter. I thank You for watching over us. I thank You for Your guidance, discernment, wisdom, knowledge, and understanding. I ask that You touch the heart of every reader that has their eyes laid on his book and this prayer. I plead the blood of Jesus over their mind, body, and soul. And I ask that You increase our spiritual hearing and vision so that we can hear You clearly, God, so we know whether to go left or right in our lives. We thank You now, Heavenly Father. We thank You for looking out for us, oh God, and we love You in Jesus' name we pray. Amen.

CHAPTER 6

THE BIG HOMIE & THE PROTÉGÉ

Let's take it back to 1989 when *Harlem Nights* hit the movie screens. When Quick was a young in', he ran into Sugar Ray after he knocked on the door to a gambling shack to give Mr. Ray his cigarettes. Little did he know, his life was about to change when he brought those cigarettes to Sugar Ray. Something special was chilling deep inside of Lil' Quick, and he had the heart of a go-getter, y'all. Yeah, I mean a go-getter and a hustler, but he just didn't know how to channel that energy, especially at a young age— just like many of us, if you really think about it.

Sugar Ray knew he had a diamond in the rough when Lil' Quick shot a toothless gambler when he tried to rob Sugar Ray's dice game. I remember when Quick walked into the gambling shack while the toothless cat was shooting dice. Kids obviously brought him bad luck because when he saw Lil' Quick, he said, "Man, I ain't shooting shit! I told you kids bring me bad luck. I can't stand them little bastards. Now, get the fuck out of here before I kick yo' ass!"

Y'all get the picture, right? I know y'all have seen that movie if you're reading this book. Long story short, the toothless cat got pissed off because Sugar Ray wouldn't put Lil' Quick out of the dice game, so he pulled a knife and tried to rob the game. Well, the hustler and the lion in Lil' Quick weren't having that fugazi shit. So, he shot the toothless gambler and killed him. For some reason, he felt it was his obligation to protect Sugar Ray from the lion's den. So, from then on, the rich old man took Lil' Quick in as his protégé and taught him the whole game and pretty much set him up for success.

I found myself in the lion's den when my great-grandmother (the sharecropper's daughter), my landlord, and I dove headfirst into the trucking industry without knowing anything. I had no idea how cutthroat the logistics industry was, but boy was I in for a rude awakening. When I left the streets alone, the strip club and all, I got a job at an alarm system company and stayed there for four years. I was the top rep, and I was making good money, but just like Lil' Baby says in his song, "I want some mo' and some mo." I wasn't feeling fulfilled there because I could only imagine how much money the company was making off my blood, sweat, and tears.

One day, a friend came to me and said, "Hey, Ashley, let's buy a truck." I looked at him crazy, was like, "Buy a truck? Really? We don't have any truck money!" But the Spirit in me said, "Take that idea to your great-grandmother," so I brought it to her. I also took it to my landlord, and it was a GO! They actually believed in the vision that I brought to them. Remember, y'all, I was the black sheep. And these people, these folks, believed in me; they trusted me with their money like that. I've never had anyone believe in me that way. So, we bought the truck for $50,000. I invested $2,000 because that's all I had, and they invested the other $12,000 for the down payment.

Meanwhile, I put my thinking cap on and started searching for contracts for our company. I saw that the oilfield industry was booming and trucks were making eight to fourteen thousand dollars a week. I secured a contract and we were ready to roll as soon as we closed the deal on the truck.

We finally closed the deal after a month. It took a whole month to close the deal because none of us had a CDL since we didn't drive trucks. While we closed on the truck, I was still working at the security system call center.

Having closed on the truck, it's time to find a driver. Since I had call center sales experience, my expertise was in the people business. I knew how to sell things, so I could sell a job opportunity for our trucking company. I knew I could. Why not? I searched for resources to post jobs for drivers because it was winding down for the truck to get rolling on the oilfield contract we had solidified. I posted the jobs on Indeed, Monster, and ZipRecruiter. You know, those sites are way too slow.

I reached out to the Texas Workforce Commission to find a driver in need of employment. Lo and behold, the Texas Workforce Commission called me with a driver who was ready to work. I'll never forget this man. His name was Mr. Vaughn.

On the surface, Mr. Vaughn was a fake shepherd of the Lord who gave me the illusion that he was a man of the Living God. It's so scary, y'all, how people can imitate being a team player on the Living God's team. I thought I had a good driver ready to roll on our frac sand hauling contract in the oilfield. When the "man of God" was ready to roll after we had closed the deal, and everything was ready to go, we gave this man the keys to go for orientation. We were so excited because we knew our driver was on the way to make money and make our trucking company some money.

My partners and I had gone beyond lit; we were ready to see our investment put the work in the oilfield. We calculated that it would take our driver four hours and twenty-five minutes, or five hours at the most, to arrive and call us with the orientation details. We were so excited. We waited about five hours to call and check in on him. No answer. We waited another hour, no answer, and another hour, no answer. Immediately, an eerie feeling came over me, and I knew that God would not allow what I was thinking in my head to actually happen. *This man gotta be sleeping or something!*

The next day came, and this bastard had stolen our $50,000 investment off the lot. I was more than devastated. Hell! I fell into a deep depression. I low-key wanted to commit suicide because here I was, with little to no money and no way to find our truck. Plus, my great-grandmother and landlord had trusted me with their investment, and now their money was gone down the drain.

My man was in the feds at the time, so I didn't even have him to hold me through this shit. My man did everything he could over the phone. He helped me stay sane by praying with me, praying for me, praying over the business, and sending me scriptures in the mail. He would hit all angles because he knew that's what he had to do as a man. He told me to put my big-girl panties on and stop feeling sorry for myself because God was only strengthening my legs at that time, and He still is. He was such comfort from so many miles away.

I felt my life was over, and to make shit worse, I had to be up in the morning to go to work at the alarm company call center. I went to work the next day and researched the driver that I had hired. Now, why in the hell was I sitting there doing background checks after I had already given this man the keys and not before? What I found about this man was more horrifying than I would have ever imagined. This man was a crackhead, arsonist, and a damn thief. So, here I am, sitting in a call center, making sales for someone else's company, when our $50,000 investment is in the hands of a crackhead. I quit my job and set out to find our investment.

Fast forward to a month later, the police found the truck in the hood of Dallas with no damn tires on it. The driver had stolen the tires then disconnected the ELD (electronic logging device) and finance house tracking device. Although we did get the truck back that time, it was stolen two times after that incident. So, I knew I had to get game tight in this cutthroat game. WELCOME TO THE TRUCKING INDUSTRY!

> If you think you'll reach your full potential without learning, you aren't dreaming and are deceiving yourself
> -Grant Cardone

After the hell I went through, I knew I had to find someone in the industry I could genuinely connect with. You know, like the type of person who doesn't just see a big butt and a smile, but someone who could see beyond my looks and actually want to help. So, I had to put my thinking cap on, and I started Googling and researching for more information in trucking groups, Instagram, and Facebook. I found a few popular trucking groups, so I posted a few questions, hoping to get some guidance.

I did get a lot of comments, even from the famous girl "The Trucking Guru." She actually told me, "Hey, Ashley, listen, whatever you need, I got you. Don't trust these men; they are wolves, so watch out, but I got you, though." The funny thing is, when I did reach out to her again, she never had me, but it's all good. But the big homie Aubrey did. He was in my comments so real with it that I knew I needed to connect with this cat because real recognize real. He was a country boy that did fifteen years of fed time flat. He got out and turned his life around for the greater good. He applied that hustle mentality to the trucking industry. He was a supervisor making big paper in the oilfield. He was a boss for real.

Aubrey would stay on the phone with me for hours at a time, giving me the blueprint step by step in this trucking game. He was giving me information that people hid or charged thousands of dollars for—because we all know the game is to be sold, not told, right? At least, that's what we've been programmed to believe. I wish our black race would understand that it's OK to genuinely pour into someone who wants to help themselves. God loves a cheerful giver, and it's OK to help others. I wish Black people would realize that God is our infinite source, so there is no LACK! Helping someone else will not stop their flow.

> I will heighten my life by helping others heighten theirs
> -Les Brown

Aubrey was so giving. The second time our truck was stolen, all he had to do was make a phone call, and he got our truck back that day! There was something special about Aubrey, something about him that put fear in people. He was a true big homie, and he didn't play when it came to Ashley. He even looked out for me when I couldn't pay my bills sometimes, after paying for fuel, paying our driver, and the truck's maintenance. Don't forget that the profit was split into three parts between my granny, landlord, and myself.

Aubrey was the real definition of a mentor, and I was the real definition of a true protégé. I soaked up all the game he taught me and took off with it because I knew it was valuable. I continued to follow the blueprint he taught me from hauling sand to hauling fuel locally, but one thing he never had to teach me was how to get a driver to become an employee. I had my people skills down game tight from my experience in stripping, the pimpin' and hoeing game, and the security alarm sales. I had that gift of gab! I always kept drivers, no matter what; the skill of survival was and still is embedded in me. I was always ready to execute a dog fight.

For some reason, I'd always been the type of person that found a solution even in the worst of the worst situations. I guess I got that from my great-granny because she's the same, a real pioneer woman. It's almost like I love solving problems and figuring shit out because, in those situations, I always found a solution. I don't know; call me weird, but I love the hunt! I love this! There's something about that shit that gets my blood going. You know!

I would research how to find drivers because, without them, hell, you could spend a billion dollars on trucks and not have shit because all your trucks are sitting still. So, I mastered driver recruiting and what to look for. Aubrey saw the hidden talent in me that I was perfecting, even when I couldn't pay my bills.

I was struggling and scared at the same time because going back to the alarm company, strippin', or any of that was not an option. Going back to the alarm company wasn't an option; they weren't going to see me fail there. I wasn't going back to the strip club because they would've known I failed! That wasn't an option either. If I had gone back then, that was the same thing as giving up, in my opinion. So, I continued to run the truck in the oilfield. The owner of the oil field company was Aubrey's homeboy. He had multiple trucks sitting because he had no drivers, and Aubrey told him, "Hey, man! Say, man!!

Man, you need to hire Ashley to keep drivers in your trucks so you can make some more money!"

Aubrey knew that in my situation, I needed the money for my livelihood, especially after I walked away from the call center job to run a trucking business. I was dedicated to the vision. I spent my last bag on the vision, and he knew that, so he looked out for me. He got me a recruiting job paying $50,000 a year with the oil field company I ran our trucks under. I had never made that type of money before. I'm a ninth-grade dropout, but now, it is on! Welcome to the 800-billion-dollar trucking industry without having trucks to make money! I was making more money in driver recruiting than I would ever have made with our two trucks running in the oilfield. My recruiting money was free and clear. No maintenance, driver pay, or fuel costs! It would be a long, hard road to success, but I was ready to run the ball.

Shout up to the big homie Aubrey's company, ADC&T (Aubrey Deckard Consulting and Transportation). Y'all better tap in!

PRAYER: Dear Lord, we're here today with open hands and an open heart, ready to depend on You to help us through the day and all that it will bring our way. Help us to be like Nehemiah. Help us come to You for guidance, strength, provision, and protection. As we face tough choices, hard decisions, and hard situations, help us remember our belovedness and help us remember that we are Your children and Your representative to the world around us. Help us live today in a way that brings honor to Your Holy name. In Jesus' name we pray. Amen.

CHAPTER 7

DIVORCING THE GAME NONPROFIT ORGANIZATION

Before I tell you this story, I had already asked God to touch my head, lips, and fingertips. So, that way, I can give you guys the message that He has for you. So, check this out! As I was getting drivers for the oil company that the big homie Aubrey hooked me up with, the owner was also referring me to so many other companies and telling them how I keep his trucks rolling. It got to the point where the referrals coming in became overwhelming. It was booming. I was only charging like $200 just because I needed some extra money, and I didn't know any better. But again, like my man told me when he was in the feds, "You don't realize the skill that God has personally equipped you with, and God is strengthening your legs, baby." So, I embraced it.

It was a Saturday night. I asked God, "God, is my home-based business Supreme Driver Recruiting what You want me to do?" I named it Supreme Driver Recruiting because the company that my trucks were under, and I was getting drivers for, was Supreme Sand haulers. So, I asked God about that. God told me immediately, "I want you to go to sleep, and I want you to go to the church that you hadn't been to in a while because you've been backsliding."

I asked God again, "Is this really what you want me to do?" He said the same thing. So, I went to sleep on that Saturday night. God gave me a vision and a dream that night. I'll never forget that Saturday night dream. My dream was in the same church God instructed me to go to in real life the next morning. When I walked into the church in the dream, I went to the bathroom, and there was a lady in there. She was a well-known church member.

"Hey, girl, how have you been?" I said.

"Ashley, I've been great. How have you been?" she said.

"I've been good," I replied.

"Well, girl, I just started a new job," she said. "Where did you start your new job? I'm happy for you," I said.

She looked me dead in my eyes in my dream, and she said, "I'm going to be working at a call center in Midland Odessa (which is the oilfield). I'll be working at a call center called Supreme Driver Recruiting."

Immediately after she said that, my alarm clock went off. It was time for me to go to the same church that was in my dream.

I got into my car and drove to the church that I backslid from, and I felt like I wasn't supposed to be there. And when I say backslid, I mean not praying the way I needed to, not asking God for His direction, and not listening to His voice.

On the way there, I told God, "I don't wanna do this. I backslid, and people are going to look at me crazy when I walk in. They don't know where I had been." And God said to me, "Whoever is without sin can cast the first stone." So, I knew I had to go because He spoke to me directly. And you know me; I tried to negotiate with God, but that never really works out for me too well.

I walked into the church, sat down, and got ready for the sermon. The sermon that was being taught was from Genesis, about Isaac. And the story was about digging the wells and how haters hate and will try anything to get you off track. The pastor said, "Listen, we're in a season where God is answering prayers right now, immediately!"

You know what's funny about that story in Genesis about Isaac? Isaac didn't care what anybody said negatively regarding his digging because he was going by the formula God gave him. Just like that dream God gave me the same night when I asked for it—immediately! He gave me the formula. There's something about that word "immediately" in the church that day that put a fire in my spirit.

When the Lord appeared to Isaac, He told him that He didn't want Isaac to go to Egypt; rather, He wanted Isaac to stay in Canaan. That's just like the times God wants you to be still. Have you ever thought about that? The Lord promised to bless Isaac right there where he was even in the time of the raging famine. Y'all hear what I'm saying? Where famine was raging!

Sometimes it doesn't matter how bad other people think your circumstances are when the reality may not be appealing to the eye. But when the Lord says "Be still," you do just that. God knows the outcome of His formula, so it's critical to follow His plan. And the same is true for every generation.

Don't worry about what the haters say. There have been haters since the beginning of time. Hell, we need them! Shout out to my spiritual coach, Willie Tubbs. He told me that the haters acronym is "having animosity toward everyone reaching success."

> ## The GREATEST REVENGE is MASSIVE SUCCESS
> -Les Brown

My spiritual coach put me up on game! We will have haters in each dimension we reach in life.

Isaac had major haters in the Bible. His haters wished they were as rich as he was. Isaac's neighbors were angry with him, so they filled in all of his wells after he had spent time digging them up! Isaac was grinding, really putting in that work. All the places where Isaac had dug holes to get water out of the earth, his neighbors filled them back with dirt so he wouldn't get more water out of them.

Y'all know of anyone that's tried to sabotage your vision before you even made it to success? I will ask that question again: Do y'all know of anyone who has tried to sabotage your vision before you even made it to success? Hearing God's voice and flowing in His overall plan for each generation is the most important thing in life to me. You have to listen to God. It is what it is. That's how I reached my current level of success.

> *You cannot cheat success! You gotta work for it! You gotta breathe it! Sleep it! Eat it! –Eric Thomas*

God knew that by equipping me with that message, I would be running into similar situations.

When I was down in the trenches, people would tell me, "Girl, you crazy; you still working like a dog on your so-called home-based business and can't even pay your bills. So, look at you. Who are you? The Ashley I know will get up and get some money, but you sitting here stuck! That idea is stupid, anyway; it's not going to work!

You are sowing into unprofitable ground and not getting any type of reward. How crazy are you?"

> Life is too short to worry about what others say about you.
> Have fun and give them something to talk about.
> -Kevin Hart

I remember the pastor's words that morning when I got my second confirmation from God. "God is responding to prayers immediately in this season." I replayed that in my head every time the haters would say negative things about my grind for the vision. And he was right because I got three confirmations in less than twelve hours! I'll run back the three confirmations for you real quick:

Number one, the dream God gave me the night I prayed and asked if Supreme Driver Recruiting was what He wanted me to turn into a business. He delivered the vision on that same night.

Number two, God telling me on the way to church not to be ashamed of going back to church because I had backslid. God repeated his Word to me in the car on the way to church, which was John 8:7. He said, "He who is without sin can cast the first stone."

And number three, the pastor saying, "God is responding to prayers immediately in this season."

After the three confirmations, I knew then that God wanted me to make my recruiting service a business. So, I took off from there with nothing but faith, and Supreme Driver Recruiting was born that day.

> I can't go back and change the hands of times but what I can do is create a new legacy -Eric Thomas

I stayed in the trenches for about five years. Even though folks told me how stupid and crazy I was to have continued pushing, even though I couldn't even pay my bills, I knew God didn't trust me for nothing. I had to keep going, no matter what my reality was.

See, it's hard being a visionary, especially when you can see where God is taking you. It's hard having to wake up with the reality of certain circumstances, but God's strength is everything! I pushed and pushed and finally got a multimillion-dollar driver recruiting contract with a mega trucking company in February of 2020. We made $30k our first month! I had never seen that kind of money before. I was so happy and thankful, then BOOM! COVID-19 hit the next month in March, and everything shut down. At this time, my man was home from the feds. He was transitioning over into the trucking industry, and we just couldn't believe that this had happened, but we were strong and made it through.

I'm here to tell you that Supreme Driver Recruiting is now the first black woman-owned call center in the United States and more prosperous than we've ever been. It took four years to get here. Business is a dog fight. We stayed in the trenches during COVID-19, and we got out of it. We were a team; he held me down, and I held him down. That's what relationships are about.

At the end of 2020, I opened up a physical call center.

That's the vision that God has brought to pass.

I wanted to give back to the community, so I hired felons. I wanted to help them transition and change their lives for the greater good. We had hourly pay, $17 to $54 an hour, which is unheard of. I came from a call center background, and I wanted to develop a call center where I would've enjoyed working.

Let me tell you how crazy and weird it may seem to the human eye how God can build your strength in a manner that you don't even understand. Many say, "God, how can you allow me to go through this?" We hired over fifteen W2 employees that I gave a shot to a better life, and they betrayed me. When I caught COVID, I left my operation in the hands of the supervisor and management. I found out that the management was sleeping with employees and allowing the business that I sacrificed my blood, sweat, and tears for to go down the drain. Employees were stealing from us, taking customers' payments through their Cash App. To make matters worse, my own family, my own sister and cousin, was stealing from the business. Now Supreme Driver Recruiting is the most profitable we've ever been.

But it's all good, though, because, who would've thought that this black girl that got abandoned by her mother and her father, a ninth-grade dropout, a former stripper, and a drug dealer, would end up in *Forbes* magazine and *Essence* magazine?

We are now creating multiple six-figure-income earners at our driver recruiting call center. My first student grossed over half a million dollars her first year!!! She was very intentional and deliberate with the tools in hand and was coachable.

Let me tell you how my God works. He's very mysterious, and that's what makes God fun. He's very spontaneous! I love that about God. You know, we fired over fifteen people, and now I see the whole vision of what God had in store for me. God is so mysterious and off the chain. I remember not too long ago when I was supposed to go out of town. We were about to miss our flight to support some of our friends. We got frustrated and decided not to go because we were running late, and out of the blue came a phone call from the city council after hours. I answered because I thought something had to be terribly wrong for the Arlington City Council to be calling me on a Friday after 5 p.m.

"Hey, Ashley, I know it's late, but we would love to send a car service to pick you up and bring you to our skybox at the Texas Ranger Stadium. We want you to meet all of the board members of the city council," the gentleman said.

This is why I believe God is mysterious and spontaneous. The doors continue to open up for me even when one closes. Now, I have created a nonprofit organization with The Supreme Team mentorship program that helps former and current exotic dancers, drug dealers, scammers, and pretty much anyone trapped in the nightlife who think there is no way out. This is to assist them with transitioning into a more professional setting in the 800-billion-dollar trucking industry. And immediately, they will have the opportunity to make $10k to $30k straight out of the gate to maintain that previous standard of living.

You know, if my man can do it, anybody can do it. I'm so proud of him because he has transitioned from that street-life hustle mindset and rechanneled it into a professional career in the trucking industry, making the same type of bread he's used to without risking his freedom.

PRAYER: Heavenly Father, I thank You for Your strength and empowerment in me as well as wisdom.

I thank You so much, God, for the harvest. I thank You for what I have and for what I will receive. I pray with gratitude and thanksgiving in my heart, Heavenly Father.

You make the rough way smooth, Heavenly Father. And I thank You for providing my every need.

I am your child, Father, and I am inspired by You every day. And I place all that I have in Your keeping, oh Lord. I plead the blood of Jesus over everybody who touches this book, reads this book, or even just sees the title of this book in the libraries, prisons, or online.

Heavenly Father, I ask You to help us prosper always, and I pray that Your light guides us. I ask that You bountifully supply our every need, dear God. I believe that we, as children of God, have the right to prosper. You and I, whoever is listening; we have the right to prosper as King's kids.

We know that You are our endless source of supply and that every good thing that comes to us directly is from You. We, as children of God, do not operate in lack because that is not of You. And we pray that You'll open Your hands, Heavenly Father, today and supply us with every good thing needed in our lives. Supply our life God with courage, strength, wisdom, guidance, and knowledge, and fill our minds, Heavenly Father, with wealth. Empower us, Heavenly Father. And we connect with You now, Heavenly Father. We thank you so much. And it is so. In Jesus' name we pray. Amen!